Inspiration

A Collections of Daily Devotions, Inspirational Stories, and Prayers

Ann Clay

DEDICATION

This book is dedicated to my ancestors, whose prayers have covered me through this journey. For I know, that without their faith, their teachings, and their unwavering prayers, I would not be in the purpose for which God has created me in the first place. I am so very blessed.

Acknowledgment

Sometimes hindsight gives us a clear picture of how faithful
God has been. We are tempted during a crisis to wonder if
God will be faithful to His promises. We focus on our
problems and our trust in God begins to waiver. We must,
however, hold on to His promise, because He will never forget
His promise to us. (2 His Promises)
The awesome power of God to create is not mine, but His -
and His alone.

I've come to truly appreciate my family and friends. My
children, Nikisha, Quetta, Chelsea, and Brian are wonderful
young people. It is my prayer that they remember and exercise
faith to help them through this challenging thing we call life.

I'm so blessed to have supportive friends who consistently
inspire me. I especially appreciate my good friends, Donna
Miller and Royce Morton for their help with this project.

I acknowledge my faith verbally and hopefully in the things I
do and say, and by associating myself with people of the same
faith and beliefs.

My Christian growth I contribute to the steady, faith-based-
teachings from my foundation, New Life in Christ Church.

I acknowledge all of you because you are the souls of my
writing passions. God granted me this gift that I might bring
you closer to him. Wherever you are in your faith, I hope that
my testimony will help you in your journey. It is my heartfelt
effort to bring truth and understanding with the words on
these pages. It is with humility, that I thank you for allowing
me to be a part of your journey to Christ.

No matter how well we try to walk right, life on earth can toss
a dynamite in our walk with God, no matter how well we try to
walk right.
Continue to be encouraged, to create a true and meaningful
relationship with God.

Romans 15:13 says, "May the God of hope fill you with joy
and peace as you trust in him, so that you may overflow with
hope by the power of the Holy Spirit."

Be Blessed!

Then we can thank God for His provision and His promises
that remind us of who we are in Him.
How? With second doses of motivation.

Lord, my ultimate desire is to know You and serve You in this world so as to spend eternity with You in the next. Sometimes my own beliefs, opinions, and desires get in the way of knowing Your will. Please send Your Holy Spirit to conform my will to Yours.

Be Kind

Growing up, it was normal in our house to have breakfast for dinner every now and again. It was quick and easy to prepare, did the same if not better job than liver and onions. Of course, I loved liver and onions, my siblings not so much.

One night, in particular, I remember my mother did exactly that after a long, hard day at work. She made breakfast for dinner. Once she was done, she placed a plate of eggs, sausage, and burnt canned biscuits on the table. I remember looking from one sibling to the other, waiting to see if anyone noticed, even though none of us would have uttered a single word. My mother didn't tolerate backtalk and would have sent us to bed without dinner, even the burnt biscuits.

Well, Daddy reached for a biscuit, smiled at my Momma, and then asked us about our day at school. I don't remember what I told him, but I watched him smear butter and jelly on that ugly, disfigured, burnt biscuit, and he ate every bite of that thing like it was the best bread ever. He never made a face nor uttered a word about it!

After we cleared the table, of course, it was my turn to do the dishes; I heard Momma apologize to my dad for burning the biscuits. I will never forget what he said. "Bae, I love burnt biscuits now and then."

Later that night, I went to kiss Daddy good night, and because I was a curious kid, I asked him if he really liked his biscuits burnt. He pulled me close, placed a light kiss on my forehead, and said, "Your Momma put in a long, hard day at work today, and she's real tired. Besides, a little burnt biscuit never hurt nobody! Now go on, Sha, we got an early day tomorrow."

As I've grown older, I think about that night all the time. Life is full of imperfect things, imperfect circumstances, and imperfect people. We should remember to be kinder to one another because we truly don't know what type of day they've had or what situation they may be going through.

I know I'm not the best at hardly anything. I'm quick to forget birthdays and anniversaries. I'm always in a rush or late for something or another. I drop stuff, burn stuff, waste stuff, just like everyone else. But what I've acknowledged over the years is that learning to accept each other's faults or misgivings, and instead, choosing to celebrate each other's differences is by far one of the most important keys to creating a healthy, growing, and lasting relationship with anyone.

And that's my prayer for you today, this year, this century—that you will learn to take the good, the bad, and the ugly parts of your life and lay them at God's feet. In the end, He's the only One able and willing to give you a relationship where a burnt biscuit isn't a dealbreaker!

This concept is relatable to your relationship with God, but it also extends to relationships with your family, friends, church members, coworkers, and people you greet.

Never put the key to your happiness in someone else's pocket - keep it in your own. You are the responsible one, and taking it out on others only harms your chances of experiencing the kind of fruitful relationships God intended for you in the first place.

God's Calling

We can forget or reject God. We can establish idols for ourselves; we can come up with our own ideas about the meaning of human existence, but God remains ever present, tirelessly calling each individual to an encounter with His purpose for our lives.

We struggle to discern, often overthinking God's will or calling for us. For those whose faith waivers from time to time or from place to place, it's harder to gauge who we are listening to. Then, some have no idea where to start when it comes to recognizing and then working within their purpose.

Calling is an expression of faith, a divine influence, an assignment that typically relates to purpose and meaning for our lives and can only come from God.
In the Bible, the word "call" is used to refer to God's initiative to bring people to Christ and to have them participate in His redemptive work within the world.

We are all called by God to a specific, unique purpose. We won't receive a voicemail, a text, or even a Facebook posting. We will, however, if we are in a relationship with God, a certainty, uniquely attuned precisely to us.

Not everyone is called to do the same things for the same reasons, nor will our purpose be a struggle because God doesn't work in indecisiveness. Everything He creates works in a manner which is guided with excellence and joy.
Paul says in 1 Corinthians 7:20: "Each one should remain in the condition in which he was called." In other words,

not everyone was called to be an evangelist or psalmist. So, stay in your lane; otherwise, you risk operating outside of the will of God. He will not call you to do something that He has not gifted you to do.

God provides varied grace incarnated in human personalities, for which we work for the good deeds of others. We do it generously, with compassion, and with purpose. When God moves us into mission mode, He gives us recurring and growing interest and awareness. The desire to work is what God uses to draw us into purpose.

Our calling is closer than we think. God will speak to our destiny. We should remain aware of what gets us excited and what drives our interests, our passion. Prayer for purpose is unceasing and will provide the assurance needed.

However, beware. Even when we know what our calling is, disappointments, doubts, and haters can easily creep into that space we call faith. That's why we should partner with someone to hold us accountable, someone with our best interest at heart, someone concerned about our relationship, our walk with God. Encouragement, support, and prayer will exhort the work of the kingdom.

Act, contribute to things other than ourselves, live in the present, end a sense of entitlement, and connect to something larger than ourselves if we want to successfully discover and fulfill our purpose. To do this, work through failures and victories, build habits that lead to joy.

Understand that this will be a journey, one that might last a lifetime, but must be realized and fulfilled. Build relationships, be accountable, expunge hate from our hearts, forgive ourselves and others, and listen obediently.

God has given us what we need to begin living in His will and pursuing our calling now.
If we truly love God, we want to always glorify Him the most. We want to be celebrated in His love, above all things.

Breakthrough

Ever been in a tough situation or waiting on God for something you've been fasting and praying for a long time? Ever wonder what are the signs when you are closer to your breakthrough with God?

At some point in our lives, we may have questioned things we thought we knew about our very existence, our purpose. Many have, and they are definitely not alone. Still, we mustn't lose hope. God has promised to answer when we persevere.

The work of God is in His timing and not our own. Some of our most noted characters in the Bible asked for big things. In some cases, they had to wait a long time to receive their answers. We know the stories of Abraham, Joshua, and Hannah. They waited for years to hear from God as they prayed unceasingly.

We pray, but prayer is not magic. Our job is to ask, in earnest, with true hearts, and reverence. It is not to dictate or control God's answer or will. We must let God be God, waiting in patience while He does His work perfectly. It requires total faith.

We do have help, and we are not in the process alone. The Holy Spirit intercedes for us with groanings far too deep for words (Romans 8:26). He is praying the perfect will of God, and we are invited to agree with Him. When we truly pray in the Holy Ghost, we surrender our agendas and let Him pray through us. And this takes us deeper with God.

What we may not know or understand is that this process is not for those of faint heart, little faith, or patience. Matthew 7:8 says: "For everyone who asks, receives, and he who seeks finds, and to him who knocks it will be opened." However, the verbs used implies constant asking, seeking, knocking, and yes, praying.

Our prayers must be persistent, specific, and with open hearts. When we feel faint, press forward in faith, and the Holy Spirit will provide strength. Keep asking, seeking, and knocking. Don't give up. Stand fast and endure the storm. Our breakthrough is closer than we think.

Like Christ

One of the most effective ways to show people how faith brings true freedom is through the witness-value of devoting one's life to witnessing, sharing the word of God.

Simply sharing our stories, our testimonies can help others going through something, even if it's something different. Our willingness to wait faithfully on God shows just how much we trust God.

Telling others how we've overcome, sharing what faith is, and how it has changed us, bears witness that we love God. Sometimes people need to see us in our commitment, allowing God's faithfulness to witness to others through us.

We may very well be the only evidence of God they may ever see, and that is why we must be responsive in our daily walk.

Sometimes we have to meet people where they are, which may not be in a church structure or any other physical representation of Christianity and spirituality.

How we live, speak, respond, or obey may be exactly what's needed to motivate faith or bring people closer to Christ. Never shrink from the ability to be the tool God uses to do His work in the earth. After all, we have the greatest example of how God has already done this exact thing through His Son, Jesus Christ.

Each Day is a Blessing

We are called to love God and one another. That is our primary vocation. The reason we rise in the morning and the purpose of our lives on earth is to learn how to receive God's love and then share it. God's gift of life to us each morning is a sign that He has a mission for us each day.

Our world is evolving to a place, not uncommon to the biblical days, where hate, greed, sickness, and faithlessness covered many parts of the world. And, in God's eyes and nose, the sores and stench of man have given humans the ability of choice; although no man is righteous, he has the choice to obey.

To obey, or not to obey, is still a blessing, and how and what we choose will be judged accordingly.
So many are lost or don't care to know God. Still, God has great love and faith in us, giving us a chance every day, an opportunity to experience His grace, a chance to love and respect, and are given provisions to live peacefully and fulfilled. Still, it's left up to us to agree with His Will.

Let us be mindful of the blessings granted us each day. They set us apart as the children of God, His to experience each day as a blessing.

Accepting Reality

God calls us who we are with all our deficiencies and difficulties. We are not immaculately conceived. No matter, we are what we are, and it is only when we accept our own reality, as Mary accepted hers, that God can draw us into his fulfillment.

He has created each of us uniquely and lovingly as He wants us. Our ability to unconditionally value all parts of who we are will help to dispel lies we tell ourselves. We are and will forever be what He intended.

The sooner we accept it, the sooner we acknowledge our understanding of His love. Practice radical honesty, own all mistakes and outcomes, resist fear, and give up chasing endless goals that will never bring us joy. That's accepting reality.

Duality resides in every life experience. Every problem has a solution, every obstacle an opportunity, and every negative a positive. How we choose to deal with these experiences speaks well to how we depend on God to shape our realities.
Reality is truth and implies abstractions in our daily lives. For example, sin is truth, but so is good.

Because we live in a secular world, the unbalance of faith can impose behaviors and thoughts that interfere with acceptance. As Christians, our underlying belief is that reality, both human and non-human, is God's creation. Possibilities are completely within His powers.

His challenge is not one we should meet alone. Never place boundaries God's grace, power, or love to the limitations of our reality. He is limitless in all He does in all He is. His path may not be our choice.

Wait Not in Restlessness

"But they that wait upon the Lord shall renew their strength; they shall mount up with wings as eagles; they shall run, and not be weary, and they shall walk, and not faint."
Isaiah 40:31

At times, we may feel so worn out and stressed, not sure we can take another step. We spend all of our time running from crisis to crisis and are constantly giving our time and energy to others. The Lord wants to renew our strength and enable us to enjoy the abundant life He intends for each one of us. The key is to wait upon Him to do so.

Our generation does not enjoy waiting. We are harried by all the commitments we have made, and the many responsibilities we hold. We rush through our lives without stopping to evaluate our activities. Sometimes, in our haste to get on with our work, we race ahead of God. Part of God's restoration process is to slow us down and make us listen to Him. As we wait on Him, God will remind us of our utter dependence upon His strength. When we slow down and seek His will, He will reveal His plans.

Biblically, waiting on the Lord is never passive; it is always active. Waiting requires us to cease our own pursuits and give God our complete attention. We may have to give up some of the activities we have allowed to inundate our lives. We need to take an entire day to sit quietly before the Lord. If we ask Him, God will show us the resources He has provided to help with the work we have been attempting on our own. God may address feelings of guilt that have motivated us to do things He has not asked us to do.

Jesus carried more responsibility than we do. More people needed Him than will ever need us. Yet, He is never overwhelmed or inadequate for the task. Now Christ offers to guide us so that we will fulfill the Father's will and gain the strength necessary for each day. (Matthew 11:28)

No Balance

Imagine you had a bank account that deposited $86,400 each morning. The account carries over no balance from day to day, allows you to keep no cash balance, and every evening cancels whatever part of the amount you had failed to use during the day. What would you do? Draw out every dollar each day!

We all have such a bank. Its name is Time. Every morning, it credits us with 86,400 seconds. Every night it writes off, as lost, whatever time we have failed to use wisely. It carries over no balance from day to day. It allows no overdraft, so we can't borrow against ourselves or use more time than we have. Each day, the account starts fresh. Each night, it destroys an unused time. If we fail to use the day's deposits, it's our loss, and we can't appeal to get it back.

There is never any borrowing time. We can't take a loan out on our time or against someone else's. The time we have is the time we have, and that is that. Time management is ours to decide how we spend the time, just as with money, we decide how we spend the money.

It is never the case of us not having enough time to do things, but the case of whether we want to do them and where they fall in our priorities.

God is Faithful

Faithful is He that calleth you, who also will do it.

(1 Thessalonians 5:24)

God never calls us to do anything without faithfully keeping His word and enabling us to do it. We are not always faithful to do what God tells us, but He remains faithful and stands by His word to fulfill what He has promised.(Isaiah 46:11)

When the children of Israel reached the Red Sea, they might have concluded that God had abandoned His promise to them. The sea was barring their advance, and the murderous Egyptian army was racing to overtake them! Yet, God proved then, as He has ever since, that He is absolutely faithful to every word He speaks to His children.

God may have spoken to you about something in particular—a ministry in your church, the way to raise your children, or what you should do in your job. You have obeyed Him, but now, you face a Red Sea Experience. It seems what you thought God wanted to accomplish is not happening. Perhaps your ministry has not been well received, or your children are rebelling, or those at your workplace are criticizing your actions. Trust in the character of God. It is His nature to be faithful.

The testimony of His people throughout the ages is expressed by the psalmist, who declared, "I have been young, and now I am old; yet, I have not seen the righteous forsaken, nor his descendants begging for bread." (Psalms 37:25)

Regardless of how bleak your present circumstances are, do not lose hope. No one has ever experienced unfaithfulness on God's part! Allow time for God to reveal His faithfulness to you. Someday you will reflect on what God has done and praise Him for His absolute faithfulness to you.

Trust in the Lord: Take everything to God in prayer.

(Proverbs 29:25)

Dear Lord, I thank You for this day.

I thank You for my being able to see and to hear this morning. I'm blessed because You are a forgiving God and an understanding God.

You have done so much for my family and me, and Lord, You continue to bless me.

Forgive me this day for everything I have done, said, or thought that was not pleasing to You.

I ask now for Your forgiveness. Please keep me safe from all danger and harm.

Help me to start this day with a new attitude, plenty of gratitude, and faith.

Let me make this the best day of my life to clear my mind so that I can hear from You.

Please, broaden my mind and my spirit so that I can accept all things that come from You.

Help me to not whine and whimper over things I have no control over.

And give me the best response when I'm pushed beyond my limits. I know that when I can't pray, You will listen to my heart.

Continue to use me to do Your will. Continue to bless me so that I may be a blessing to others.

Keep me strong so that I may help the weak.

Keep me uplifted so that I may have words of encouragement for others.

I pray for those who are lost and can't find their way.

I pray for those who are misjudged and misunderstood.

I pray for those who don't know You intimately.

I pray for those who don't believe. But I thank You that I believe You change people and You change things.

I pray for all my children, sisters, and brothers, for every family member, for peace, love, and joy in their homes, and that they are out of debt and all their needs are met.

I pray they all know that there is no problem, circumstance, or situation greater than You, God.

Every battle is in Your hands for You to fight. God, I love You; I need You, please, come into my heart.

In Jesus' name. Amen!

Prayer is Universal

Prayer can be a way to determine who we are, in understanding who created us, and how we obtain our identity. May we find fulfillment in who we are by spending time in communion with Christ through prayer. *Dear Heavenly Father, may my deliberate act of praying renew my relationship with You so that all will know and see You in me; and therefore, desire to seek You.*

Jesus' New Command

Christ gave His followers, including us, a powerful new commandment that, if obeyed, would set us apart from the rest of the world.

"As I have loved you, so you must love one another. If you have love for one another, then everyone will know that you are my disciples." (John 13:34-35)

How we treat fellow Christians in public is a sign not only that we are converted, but we are also mature in the faith. Just like faith, love without works is spiritually dead. True love must be demonstrated consistently by how we live our lives. Hate has no place in the life of a Christian. To the degree in which we hate is the degree to which we are still immature.

The Definition of Spiritual Maturity

Paul teaches us what maturity on a spiritual level is and is not. To paraphrase what he says in 1 Corinthians 13:4-8, it states, the real love of God is patient, kind, does not envy or brag, or is full of vanity. It does not behave rudely, nor is it selfish, nor is it easily provoked. Godly love never rejoices in sin but always does so regarding the truth. It bears all things and believes all things, hopes all things, endures all things.

Since the love of God never fails, His love within us projected to others ought to not fail either.

The person who has reached a measure of spiritual maturity is not preoccupied with self. Those who are mature have come to a level where they're no longer interested in the sins of others (1Corinthians 13:5). They no longer keep a record, as Paul put it, of the sins committed by others.

Mature spiritual believers rejoice in the truth of God. They pursue truth and let it take them to wherever it leads.

Mature believers have no desire to indulge in evil, nor do they try to take advantage of others when they indulge in it. They are always working to remove the spiritual darkness that engulfs the world and to protect those who are vulnerable to its dangers. Those who are mature Christians, dedicate time to pray for others. *"And we urge you, brothers and sisters, warn those who are idle and disruptive, encourage the disheartened, help the weak, be patient with everyone."*

(1 Thessalonians 5:17)

Love enables us to persevere and have hope in what God can do. Those who are mature in the faith are friends to others, not only in the good times but also the bad.

Having spiritual maturity involves being sensitive to the power and leadership of God's spirit. It offers us the ability to possess the same kind of agape love as God. As we grow in grace and knowledge and obey God with our whole heart, His Spirit grows as well (Acts 5:32).

The Apostle Paul prayed that the believers in Ephesus be filled with Christ and comprehend the multiple dimensions of his divine love. (Ephesians 3:16-19) God's Spirit in us makes us His chosen people (Acts 1:8).

It gives us the ability to overcome and be victorious over our self-destructive human nature. The more of God's Spirit we have, the faster we will become the spiritually mature Christians God desires for all is children.

Faith and Trust in God

Sometimes we forget who's in charge. We fret about the future and nurture past hurts. Mary's example reminds us how much simply being present and attentive can be to those in our lives who are hurting—and of our need to turn over the hard tasks to God. To do so requires faith and trust in God.

The difference between faith and trust are often used interchangeably as if they are the same. However, they are not the same. Faith recognizes that the world is more than about us; it is about connecting power, which links us to God and makes Him assessable, especially when we need him most.

Faith is the basic ingredient to begin a relationship with God. Faith helps build an understanding that there are things we will never have control over, and being okay with that because God will provide. To live by faith requires living by faith, as said in 2 Corinthians 5:7, "For we live by faith and not by sight." In essence, when things are not moving in our lives, trusting that God is setting up the opportunity for us to trust that He will come through and provide something even better than we expected.

On the other hand, trust is based largely on evidence that is real, according to the senses and human reason. We live in a world where trust is in short supply, having dealt with disappointment and misfortune so often, it is hard to rely solely on anyone or anything. We're often trying to fix things ourselves, interfering with God's great plans for us. Even amid turmoil, God sticks with us and uses those challenges to shape us.

To trust God requires us to be secure, fearing nothing, and relying purely on hope, being solely aligned with God's intentions when it comes to our wellbeing. Sometimes trusting Him completely is tough, and we forget that living the life God intends for us means resting solely and comfortably in Him.

To do so, we must surrender to God with our thoughts and words, acknowledging Him always, praying, and admitting that our humanness is no match for His awesome and limitless powers. When we pray, we must admit that our burdens are more than we can handle, and ask that He relieves us from our troubles. We must also understand there are no timetables, no microwave fixes, no control, or worry involved.

The world can clutter our relationship with God. However, when we remember that our lives work best when God provides our every need, we gain faith and trust.

Even when we fail, if we place complete trust in God, He will never disappoint us, never leave us, and will always, and completely be faithful to us because He is trustworthy.

Relationship

The Lord opposes anything that hinders our relationship with Him (Deuteronomy 6:15). He knows the danger of other gods, how they will lure us away, deceive us, and leave us empty. He will tolerate nothing that takes precedence over our love for Him. Our faithfulness to God assures us of the abundant life He wants to give us. If we reject Him, He will pursue us until we return to Him.

We should not resent the fact that God wants to guard our relationship with Him. It should bring us comfort. Our relationship with God should be our top priority. It should dictate how we spend our time, our money, and our energy. If certain people or our possessions separate us from God, we must reexamine our hearts and give our devotion first to Him as He commands.

God wants each of us to love Him with all of our heart, mind, soul, and strength (Mark 12:30). Our love for God should extend to every corner of our lives. God loved us so much that He gave us His own Son. Let us respond by giving Him our highest devotion in return.

Giving Your Best

"Do not sacrifice to the LORD your God an ox or a sheep that has any defect or flaw in it, for that would be detestable to him."
(Deuteronomy 17:1)

God's love moved Him to sacrifice that which meant the most to Him—His only Son. Our response, if we truly understand His love for us, is the desire to give back to God that which means the most to us.

The Old Testament reveals that God set forth high standards for the sacrifices He required of His people. A worthy sacrifice had to cost the people something. As their hearts shifted away from God, the people began struggling to give God costly offerings. They brought blind, lame, and sick animals, assuming God could not tell the difference (Malachi 1:8). God saw what they were doing and declared their offerings to be in vain (Malachi 1:10). Throughout the Old Testament period, God was setting the stage for the ultimate, perfect, and sinless sacrifice of His Son for the sins of humanity.

The offerings we give back to God reveal our hearts' condition. A heart that overflows with gratitude for God's love will respond in selfless devotion. If we are unwilling to sacrifice our time, possessions, money, or energy, we reveal that we do not love God as He desires, showing we lack obedience.

God takes delight in the person who gives to Him cheerfully out of a loving heart, a person who understands that God is the source of everything he has

and who knows that God will more than compensate for whatever is sacrificed for Him. (2 Corinthians 9:8)
If you struggle in giving your best offerings to God, pause, and reflect on what God sacrificed for you. To be obedient, trust Him and give Him the best you have because you love Him with all your heart.

Giving God Our All

For those who live in friendship with God, it is natural to praise, thank, repent, and yes, even to tell him of our grief and our sufferings. Giving our all builds the timeless relationship with God that brings understanding and promotes His glory.

To promote God's glory, we must honor Him by giving Him the best of our lives, even in our challenging times. To give our all means to sacrifice the things we want to praise God. However, God doesn't want or expect us to do stupid things or give our lives or take the lives of others.

Whether spiritual or physical, every ability, talent, strength, and skill we possess, have been given and ordained to us by God. If we believe this, the least we can do is use whatever He has given us for His glory.
It's nice when our plans and God's plans for us agree, but that doesn't always happen. Sometimes we will have to leave our plans at the cross if we plan to follow Christ and do what He created us to do, giving our all and our very best.

It is important to develop the habit of looking to the Holy Spirit for direction in our home lives and career choices, and even our volunteerism, to make certain we are doing what He has called us to do with our talents, our gifts.

Sometimes the only way to find out why we were given certain gifts and talents, we have to actually use them; of course, we need to use them to benefit others and, more importantly, God's will. Gifts and talents sometimes come easy, but most times are things we make a sacrifice to do, something outside of our comfort, abilities, or willingness to choose to do.

Understand that if by chance, we head in the wrong direction, the Lord will reveal the missteps and make adjustments. How? With your steadfast agreement to listen and willingness to obey.

Exactly how do you plan your time to ensure you are putting it to the best use? Begin every day by prayerfully giving your time to God.

It's Time

"Another of His disciples said to Him, "Lord, let me first go and bury my father." (Matthews 8:21)

Often, our struggle, as Christians, is not in deciding whether we should obey Christ, but whether we do it immediately. We know to follow Christ and commit ourselves to do what He has told us. Yet, often, we are slow to obey! God's revelation of His will is His invitation for us to respond immediately.

Some would-be disciples pledged their willingness to follow Jesus, but they told Him they were not ready yet. In Jesus' day, a Jewish man was expected to care for his elderly parents until they died. One man wanted to wait until his father died before going with Jesus. This would be an honorable delay.

The man had to choose between this important responsibility and heeding a call from the Lord. Yet, God knew this man, and He knew the man's father. God would have taken care of the man's father if he only would have followed Jesus. This was an opportunity to walk with the Son of God; yet, the concerns of this life were competing for priority with obedience to God.

Timing our obedience is crucial. Invitations from God come with a limited opportunity to respond. Some opportunities to serve Him, if not accepted immediately, will be lost. Occasions to minister to others may pass us by. When God invites us to intercede for someone, it may be critical that we stop what we are doing and immediately adjust our lives to what God is doing.

Missing opportunities to serve the Lord can be tragic. When an invitation comes from God, the time to respond is now.

Life's Challenges

Life's challenges sometimes seem impossible. Do you feel you are too weak to fight the battle? Don't give up! Keep your heart loyal to God, for He constantly watches over you, and He desires to demonstrate His strength in your life. God is willing and just as capable of giving you victory in your current challenge as He was with those in times past. The question is not whether God is looking for His people, but whether His people are seeking Him.

Take comfort in God's promise that He watches over you, and He wants to give you victory.

Making Peace

We are not at peace with others because we are not at peace with ourselves; we are not at peace with ourselves because we are not at peace with God.

The very things we hold close to our hearts, the things that linger in our minds, are the things that compete with God's desire for our attention and our rest within Him. How can we make peace, when we hold on to things that put distance between us and others? Better yet, how do we keep peace with God when we attempt to hide in the distance from Him?

The opportunity to live in harmony first rests in our own inner peace, the ability to love and respect others, and to expect it not just from others, but expect it of ourselves as well. To do this, interchangeably requires a greater power of love and faith that places us under the watchful, prayerful, and constant peace with God.

Peace begins with an overwhelming desire, a yearning to live and forgive, to place our trust in love, understanding, self-reflection, prayer, and grace.

Love one another as He loves us. We don't always get it right. We don't always react kindly when others betray us and intentionally hurt us. The energy required to be in conflict is far greater than seeing past our differences.

Champions of God's Love

"The LORD will march out like a champion, like a warrior he will stir up his zeal; with a shout he will raise the battle cry and will triumph over his enemies." (Isaiah 42:13)

God has given us the heart of a champion far beyond any endeavor that might be accomplished... nor our worries about tomorrow— not even the powers of hell can separate us from God's love.

Champions are resilient believers, surpassing all elements standing in an uncharted path, seeking understanding, building strength through sacrifice, practice, support, and thoughts, and has passion, faith, and discipline.

Throughout the Bible, God gives us great examples of people championing his love— people who displayed amazing faith in Him —Moses, Abraham, and David to name a few.

Residing in the absolute care of God requires both faith and obedience; both are challenging tasks for all living creatures on this earth. However, as we live in the world, the need to champion God's love requires faith that transcends into worry-free living, even in a world where God is socialized as a craze that requires things seen to win beliefs.

In this microwave world, inundated with Google, social media likes and followers, where everything is politically correct, where behaviors and ungodliness are acceptable and acknowledged, it's any wonder how anyone can champion God's love. The things we see and do, worldly behaviors, the sinful behaviors, are all the things God hates.

How can we love God or champion Him if we blatantly and continuously ignore all He says is righteousness? How can we say we love God while abandoning every good He represents? It can't be so! This fake love will only remove His purpose for our lives.

Romans 12:9 says, "Love must be sincere. Hate what is evil and cling to what is good."

In today's world, laws, society, and leaders have made the difference between good and bad blurred by telling the world it's okay to be and do all the things God has commanded us not to do. To the average believer and the unbelievers, this nonsense gives them a reason to continue to turn away from God. Society has generated ungodly behaviors, attitudes, beliefs, making unbiblical behavior now acceptable, the law of the land, and a way of life.

History seems to repeat itself because what we're seeing is no different from a time in biblical days when the world allowed sin to rule, and God had to step in.

In order to champion God's love, we must do what is right and good in the sight of our Heavenly Father. God's love is a constant in our lives. We just forget because of past pain and false beliefs. It is important to understand that God's love is not defined by the way humans love. So, refrain from projecting limitations and the limitations of others onto God.

Our lives, as we know it, instantly changes when we renew our minds with the Word of God, when we choose to make champion-like decisions, rise above ordinary, and shy away from the worldly behaviors.

A champion must know he will do the right thing when the time comes.

It's more than talk and comes with an established relationship with God. To champion His unwavering love surpasses faith, obedience, and love.

Victory

When we're looking for God's favor in our situation, we must have a plan before we can declare victory. Our plan changes when God speaks.

God's plan requires us to wait until He brings things together. He wants us to depend on Him so that we can witness see how He will work things out.

When we walk in God and faith, we win, we are victorious. Faith in God's plan, even when it doesn't sound right, allows us to get into a position to get what God has in store for us. It requires action that we wait to move on.

Doing so establishes a covenant with God to create an atmosphere of success. When we agree with God's plan, our chances of victory are greater than if we attempt to do it on our own.

Signs of Maturity in Christians

The ability to display Godly love is a key sign of a mature Christian. God has called us to imitate Him. The Apostle Paul stated to the Ephesians church that they should walk or live in love just as Christ practiced when he walked the earth. (Ephesians 5:1-2)

Believers are to develop the character to love on a spiritual plane. The more of God's spirit in us, and the more we yield to its influence, the better we can love as God does. Paul wrote that God pours out the love He has into us through the effectual working of His spirit. (Romans 5:5)

Signs of Immature Christians

Many people think they have reached maturity in the faith, but in reality, they act more like little spiritual children. What reasons do people use to justify their view that they (or even someone else) are more grown up and spiritual than others?
. Being a church member for years
. Intimate knowledge of church doctrines
. Going to services every week
. Being old
. Being able to effectively put others down
. Spending time with church leaders
. Being financially well-off
. Giving significant sums of money to the church
. Knowing quite a bit about the Bible
. Dressing well for church

The Shoes - A Story Retold

Author Unknown

My alarm went off -- it was Sunday again;
I was tired -- it was my one day to sleep in.
But the guilt I'd have felt the rest of the day
Would have been too much, so I'd go; I'd pray.

I showered and shaved, adjusted suit and tie,
Got there and swung into a pew just in time.
Bowing my head in humble prayer
Before I closed my eyes,
I saw that the shoe of the man next to me
Was touching my own, and I sighed.

With plenty of room on either side, I thought,
 "Why do our soles have to touch?"
 It bothered me so; he was glued to my shoe,
 But it didn't seem to bother him much.
 Then the prayer began: "Heavenly Father," someone
said--
But I thought, "Does this man with the shoes have no
pride?"

 They were dusty, worn, scratched end to end.
 What's worse, there were holes on the side!

 "Thank You for blessings," the prayer went on.
The shoe man said a quiet "Amen."

I tried to focus on the prayer,
But my thoughts were on his shoes again.

Aren't we supposed to look our best when walking
through that door?

"Well, this certainly isn't it," I thought, glancing toward
the floor.

Then the prayer ended, and songs of praise began.
The shoe man was loud, sounding proud as he sang.
He lifted the rafters; his hands raised high;
The Lord surely heard his voice from the sky.
Then the offering was passed; what I threw in was
steep.

The shoe man reached into his pockets, so deep, and I
tried to see what he pulled out to put in, then I heard a
soft "clink," as when silver hits tin.

The sermon bored me to tears--And no lie--
It was the same for the shoe man,
For tears fell from his eyes.

At the end of the service, as is the custom here,
We must greet the visitors and show them good cheer.
But I was moved inside to want to meet this man, so
after the closing, I shook his hand.

He was old, his skin dark, his hair a mess.
I thanked him for coming, for being our guest,
He said, "My name's Charlie, glad to meet you, my
friend,"

And there were tears in his eyes--but he had a wide
grin.

"Let me explain," he said, wiping his eyes.

"I've been coming for months, and you're the first to
say, 'Hi.' I know I don't look like all the rest, but I
always try to look my best. I polish my shoes before my
long walk, but by the time I get here, they're as dirty as
chalk."

My heart fell to my knees, but I held back my tears.
He continued, "And I must apologize for sitting so near.
But I know when I get here, I must look a sight. And I
thought if I touched you, our souls might unite."

I was silent for a moment, knowing anything I said
would pale in comparison, so I spoke from my heart,
not my head.

"Oh, you've touched me," I said. "And taught me, in
part, that the best of a man is what's in his heart."
The rest, I thought, "This man will never know how
thankful I am that he touched my soul!"

Making Pancakes

Six-year-old Brandon decided one Saturday morning to fix his parents pancakes. He found a big bowl and spoon, pulled a chair to the counter, opened the cupboard, and pulled out the heavy flour canister, spilling it on the floor. He scooped some of the flour into the bowl with his hands, mixed in most of a cup of milk, added some sugar, leaving a floury trail on the floor, which by now had a few tracks left by his kitten.

Brandon was covered with flour and getting frustrated. He wanted this to be something very good for Mom and Dad, but it was getting very bad.

He didn't know what to do next, whether to put it all into the oven or on the stove, and he didn't know how the stove worked! Suddenly, he saw his kitten licking from the bowl of mix and reached to push her away, knocking the egg carton to the floor. Frantically, he tried to clean up this monumental mess but slipped on the eggs, getting his pajamas white and sticky.

And just then he saw Dad standing at the door, big crocodile tears welled up in Brandon's eyes. All he'd wanted to do was something good, but he'd made a terrible mess. He was sure a scolding was coming, maybe even a spanking. But his father just watched him. Then, walking through the mess, he picked up his crying son, hugged him, and loved him, getting his own pajamas white and sticky in the process.

That's how God deals with us. We try to do something good in life, but it turns into a mess. Our marriages get all sticky, or we insult a friend, or we can't stand our job, or our health goes sour.

Sometimes we just stand there in tears because we can't think of anything else to do.
That's when God picks us up, loves us, and forgives us, even though some of our mess gets all over Him.
But just because we might mess up, we can't stop trying to "make pancakes" for God or others. Sooner or later, we'll get it right, and then they'll be glad we tried.

How Big Is Your Storm?

A young woman went to her mother and told her about her life and how things were so hard for her. She did not know how she was going to make it and wanted to give up. She was tired of fighting and struggling. It seemed that as one problem was solved a new one arose.

Her mother took her to the kitchen. She filled three pots with water. In the first, she placed carrots in the second, she placed eggs. And in the last, she placed ground coffee beans. She let them sit and boil without saying a word.

In about twenty minutes, she turned off the burners. She fished the carrots out and placed them in a bowl. She pulled the eggs out and placed them in a bowl. Then she ladled the coffee out and placed it in a bowl. Turning to her daughter, she asked, "Tell me, what do you see?"

"Carrots, eggs, and coffee," she replied.

She brought her closer and asked her to feel the carrots. She did and noted that they were soft. She then asked her to take an egg and break it. After pulling off the shell, she observed the hard-boiled egg. Finally, her mom asked her to sip the coffee.

The daughter smiled as she tasted its rich aroma. The daughter then asked, "What's the point, mother?"

Her mother explained that each of these objects had faced the same adversity--boiling water, but each reacted differently. The carrot went in strong, hard, and unrelenting. However, after being subjected to the boiling water, it softened and became weak. The egg had been fragile. Its thin outer shell had protected its liquid interior. But after sitting through the boiling water, its inside became hardened. However, the ground coffee beans were unique. After they were in the boiling water, they actually changed the water.

"Which are you?" she asked her daughter. "When adversity knocks on your door, how do you respond? Are you a carrot, an egg, or a coffee bean?"

Think of this: Which am I? Am I the carrot that seems strong, but with pain and adversity, do I wilt and become soft and lose my strength?

Am I the egg that starts with a malleable heart, but changes with the heat? Did I have a fluid spirit, but after a death, a breakup, a financial hardship, or some other trial, that now I've become hardened and stiff? Does my shell look the same, but on the inside, am I bitter and tough with a stiff spirit and a hardened heart?

Or am I like the coffee bean? The bean actually changes the hot water, the very circumstance that brings the pain. When the water gets hot, it releases the fragrance and flavor. If you are like the bean, when things are at their worst, you get better and change the situation around you. When the hours are the darkest and trials are their greatest, do you elevate to another level?

How do you handle Adversity? Are you a carrot, an egg, or a coffee bean?

Don't tell God how big your storm is, tell the storm how big your God is!

MAYBE?

Maybe God wanted us to meet the wrong people before meeting the right one so that when we finally meet the right person, we will know how to be grateful for that gift.

Maybe when the door of happiness closes, another opens, but often, we look so long at the closed door we don't see the one which opened for us.

Maybe the best kind of friend is the kind you can sit on a porch and swing with, never say a word, and then walk away feeling like it was the best conversation you've ever had.

Maybe it is true that we don't know what we have until we lose it, but it is also true that we don't know what we have been missing until it arrives.

Giving someone all your love is never an assurance they will love you back. Don't expect love in return; just wait for it to grow in their heart; but if it does not, be content it grew in yours.

It takes only a minute to get a crush on someone, an hour to like someone, and a day to love someone; but it takes a lifetime to forget someone.

Don't go for looks; they can deceive. Don't go for wealth; even that fades away. Go for someone who makes you smile because it takes only a smile to make a dark day seem bright. Find the one who makes your heart smile.

There are moments in life when you miss someone so much that you just want to pick them from your dreams and hug them for real.

Dream what you want to dream; go where you want to go; be what you want to be because you have only one life and one chance to do it all.

May you have enough happiness to make you sweet, enough trials to make you strong, enough sorrow to keep you human, enough hope to make you happy.

Always put yourself in others' shoes. If you feel it hurts you, it probably hurts the other person, too.
The happiest of people don't necessarily have the best of everything; they just make the most of everything that comes along their way.

Happiness lies for those who have cried, hurt, searched, and tried, for only they can appreciate the importance of people who have touched their lives.

Love begins with a smile, grows with a kiss, and ends with a tear.

The brightest future will always be based on a forgotten past; you can't go on well in life until you let go of your past failures and heartaches.

When you were born, you were crying, and everyone around you was smiling. Live your life so that when you die, you are the one smiling and everyone around you is crying.

CHRIST-like WAYS TO REDUCE STRESS...

Saints should never borrow from the future. If you worry about what may happen tomorrow, and it doesn't happen, you have worried in vain. Even if it does happen, you have to worry twice. Instead:

1. Pray.
2. Go to bed on time.
3. Get up on time so you can start the day unrushed.
4. Say no to projects that won't fit into your schedule or will compromise your mental health.
5. Delegate tasks to capable others.
6. Simplify and un-clutter your life.
7. Less is more. (Although one is often not enough, two are often too many).
8. Allow extra time to do things and to get to places.
9. Pace yourself. Spread out significant changes and challenging projects over time; don't lump the hard things all together.
10. Take one day at a time.
11. Separate worries from concerns. If a situation is a concern, find out what God would have you do and let go of the anxiety. If you can't do anything about a situation, forget it.
12. Live within your budget; don't use credit cards for ordinary purchases.
13. Have backups; an extra car key in your wallet, an extra house key buried in the garden, extra stamps, etc.
14. K.M.S. (Keep Mouth Shut). This single piece of advice can prevent an enormous amount of trouble.
15. Do something for the kid in you every day.
16. Carry a Bible with you to read while waiting in line.

17. Get enough rest.
18. Eat right.
19. Get organized, so everything has its place.
20. Listen to a self-help audio while driving that can help improve your quality of life.
21. Write down thoughts and inspirations.
22. Every day, find time to be alone.
23. Having problems? Talk to God on the spot. Try to nip small problems in the bud. Don't wait until it's time to go to bed to try and pray.
24. Make friends with godly people.
25. Keep a folder of favorite Scriptures on hand.
26. Remember, the shortest bridge between despair and hope is often a good "Thank You, Jesus."
27. Laugh.
28. Laugh some more!
29. Take your work seriously, but not yourself at all.
30. Develop a forgiving attitude (most people are doing the best they can).
31. Be kind to unkind people (They probably need it the most).
32. Sit on your ego.
33. Talk less; listen more.
34. Slow down.
35. Remind yourself that you are not the general manager of the universe.
36. Every night before bed, think of one thing you're grateful for that you've never been grateful for before. God has a way of turning things around for you.

"If God is for us, who can be against us?" (Romans 8:31)

Giving Our Best

"Do not sacrifice to the Lord your God an ox or a sheep that has any defect or flaw in it, for that would be detestable to him."
(Deuteronomy 17:1)

If we are to reverence God, we should do it so as He has reverenced us. God's love moved Him to sacrifice what meant the most to Him—His Son. If we truly understand His love for us, we should desire to give back to God that which means the most to us.

God has set forth high standards for the sacrifices He required of His people. In biblical days, a worthy sacrifice had to cost the people something, something it took a long time for them to earn. But as their hearts shifted away from God, they began struggling with what to give God, especially costly offerings.

They started bringing blind, lame, and sick animals; presumptuously, believing God would not know the difference (Malachi 1:8). However, God saw their unworthy offerings and declared their contributions vain (Malachi 1:10).

He was not pleased because among them was not one sincere or honest priest. They'd become selfish and worldly, so much so that they couldn't even kindle a fire on the hearth of the altar. Their burnt offerings were not acceptable.

Throughout the Old Testament period, God was setting the stage for the ultimate, perfect, and sinless sacrifice of His Son for the sins of humanity as an example of what was expected of us.

The offerings we give back to God reveal our hearts' condition. A heart that overflows with gratitude for God's love will respond in selfless devotion. It entails building a loving and giving relationship with Him through our works, deeds, worship, and faith.

If we are unwilling to sacrifice our time, our possessions, our money, or our energy, we indicate that we do not love God as He desires. God takes delight in the person who gives to Him cheerfully out of a loving heart, a people who understand that God is the source of everything they have and knows that God will more than compensate for whatever is sacrificed for Him (2 Corinthians 9:8).

Yes, God can bless abundantly, so that all things at all times, when we need it, shall be given to us. And we will have more than enough of everything.

When we struggle to give God our best, we should pause and reflect on what God has sacrificed for us. He always gives His best to us especially when we love him with all our hearts.

God Keeps Every Promise

"Now I am about to go the way of all the earth. You know with all your heart and soul that not one of all the good promises the Lord your God gave you has failed. Every promise has been fulfilled; not one has failed." (Joshua 23:14)

Near the end of his life, Joshua took time with the Israelites to review all that God had done for them since they first began following Him. God had given them an impossible assignment: to conquer a foreign and hostile land with fortified cities and armies more powerful than their own. The Israelites were to go forward with nothing more than God's promise that He would go with them and take care of them. Joshua reminded the Israelites that God had kept every promise. They had experienced numerous victories and had enjoyed God's provision for every need.

 The truth about our covenant relationship with God is that it has responsibility, as the covenanted people of God did when they fled Egypt. Sometimes, reflection gives us a clear picture of how faithful God has been. Remember the dark days when we weren't sure God would show up, and He did.

The days when we were tempted during a crisis to wonder if God would be faithful to His promises. We focused on our problems, and our trust in God began to waver. Twenty-four years after God promised Abraham and Sarah a son, they were still waiting on God to fulfill His promise. But by year twenty-five, Abraham and Sarah understood God's faithfulness.

As David was fleeing for his life, he may have been uncertain how God would keep His promise to make him a king, but at the end of his long prosperous reign, David remembered how God had kept every promise.

His Word is true, and He never changes, despite the foolish things we often say and do. He is the unchanging and unchangeable God, who remains true to His Word, despite the faithless and ungodly ways we have often behaved. Praise God that despite our many faults and failures, we know in our hearts that God is faithful and true, and not one of His promises will ever fail - nor can they ever fail. The Word of God is tested and true. The Word of God is gracious and good. The Word of God stands fast forever, and at all times.

He is a shield to all who takes refuge in Him, and His Word is upright and just. How foolish that we do not always take Him at His Word or trust Him to keep His promises. Let us walk and worship our gracious God in spirit and truth. And let us humbly believe and obey all that He has spoken from this day forward and forevermore.

You, too, can rely on God's faithfulness. When in crisis, hold to the promise of God, who will not forget His promises to you. Look back and recount the many ways in which God has been faithful to His Word. Though no one can go back and make a brand new start, anyone can start from now and make a brand new ending.
Now, who is there to harm us if we are zealous for what is good? But even if we have to suffer for righteousness' sake, we will be blessed. Have no fear of them with minds

that are alert and fully sober, set our hopes on the grace brought to us when Jesus Christ is revealed to the world (Peter 1:13-14 (NIV).

The Lord is our armor. He will protect us from all things. Give Him thanks and pray for the guidance and strength we need today to keep any naysayers at bay.

Even if someone has only a yearning to love God, that is enough. It comes from God himself because God is present wherever there is a desire for His love. Yearn for Him always, yearn with greater confidence, and do not be afraid.

New Strength

"But those who hope in the Lord will renew their strength. They will soar on wings like eagles; they will run and not grow weary; they will walk and not be faint." (Isaiah 40:31)

At times, we may feel so worn out and stressed that we are not sure we can take another step. We often spend all of our time running from crisis to crisis and constantly giving our time and energy to others. Our God wants to renew our strength and enable us to enjoy the abundant life He intends for us. The key is to wait upon Him to do so. From earlier passage.

To wait is about binding together with Him. Those who "bind together" with Him shall renew their strength. So, what Isaiah is saying here is we're getting our strength renewed by being very close to the Lord.

In the long haul of life, the race goes to the one who can "walk and not faint," the person who can keep going, enduring, putting one foot in front of the other, not dramatically or excitingly, but with perseverance. If we can do that, we will be winners with the ability to run with vision and purpose for our lives. We know of His promises and don't lose sight of them. It means that in trial, tribulation, and sorrow, we know we serve the all-sufficient God, who is stronger than anything in this world. He has overcome.

However, our generation does not enjoy waiting. We are harried by all the commitments we have made and the many responsibilities we hold. We rush through our lives without stopping to evaluate our activities. Sometimes in our haste to get on with our work, we race ahead of God. Part of God's restoration process is to slow us down and make us listen to Him. As we wait on Him, God will remind us of our utter dependence upon His strength. When we slow down and seek His will, He will reveal His plans.

Biblically, waiting on the Lord is never passive; it is always active. Waiting requires us to cease our own pursuits and give God our complete attention. We may have to give up some of the activities we have allowed to inundate our lives. We may need to take an entire day to sit quietly before the Lord (What are you doing Saturday?). If we ask Him, God will provide us the resources needed. He will help with the work we have been trying to do on our own. God addresses feelings of guilt that have motivated us to do things that He has not asked us to do.

To wait patiently, try to occupy your time by reading Scripture, listening to Christian music, watching inspiring videos or movies, or going to sleep. If you feel yourself getting anxious or impatient, take a few slow, deep breaths to stay calm. Pray and remain focused on the positive whenever possible to make the wait more comfortable.

Jesus carried more responsibility than we do. More people needed Him than will ever need us. Yet, He was never overwhelmed or inadequate for the task. Now Christ offers to guide us so that we will fulfill our heavenly Father's will and gain the strength necessary for each day. (Matthew 11:28)

Prayer: Lord, the demands of my circumstances sometimes become more than I feel I can bear. I need new strength today to face it all. Lead me to a place of peace and rest so I can be refreshed, renewed, and restored. I won't give up, but I do want to rest, just for a while. Make it so. In Jesus' name, amen.

No weapon formed against us shall prosper! Stand fast, firmly remain in the same position and keep the same opinion, and refuse to be defeated. The Holy Spirit enables us and gives us the power to live for the Lord the life He requires from the believer or those seeking desperately to love and obey Him.

Those who Mourn

"Blessed are those who mourn, for they shall be comforted." (Matthew 5:4)

People who feel spiritual poverty, mourn after God, lamenting the sin that separated them from God's blessings. Everyone flees from sorrow, and seeks after joy; yet, true joy must necessarily be the fruit of sorrow. Only people deeply convinced of the sinfulness feel the plague of their own heart and turn with disgust from all worldly support. True happiness is why they seek God's promise of solid comfort. (Matthew 11:28)

God wants us to experience His joy (John 15:11). Yet, we cannot experience His joy until we have mourned over our sin. If we do not grieve over the weight of our sin, we have no concept of sin's devastating power. If we treat our sin lightly, we demonstrate that we have no sense of the enormity of our offense against almighty God. Our sin caused the death of God's son. It causes us to fall short of what God intends (Romans 3:23). It brings pain and sorrow to others as well as to ourselves.

The Bible says that those who grieve over their sin will draw near to God (James 4:8-10). Those who mourn and weep over their sin are in a position to repent (Luke 4:18-19). There cannot be repentance without the realization of the gravity of sin. Regret for sin's consequences is not the same as sorrow for sinning against God. Confession of sin is not necessarily an indication of repentance.

Repentance comes only when we acknowledge that our transgression has come from a heart that is far from God, and we are brokenhearted over our grievous offenses against holy God.

Jesus said that those who are heartbroken over their sin would find comfort. They will experience new dimensions of God's love and forgiveness. His infinite grace is sufficient for the most terrible sin. Do not try and skip the grieving process of repentance to move on to experience joy. God will not leave you to weep over your sin but will forgive you, comfort you, and fill you with His joy.

Made for a Purpose

Live life on purpose, not by accident.

Knowing where you came from makes a huge difference in your life. Let's say you believed you were the product of some cosmic accident. No intelligent design was involved in this world or your life. Things "just happened," and you just happen to be here. When you believe you got here by accident, you will live your life by accident. It may not seem like that to you because you'll make your plans and set your goals. But for what overall purpose?

When we know without a doubt that God made the universe and created us in His image (Genesis 1:27), we know we were made for a purpose. God is very purposeful in what He does, from every small thing to each major event in our lives. Imagine the confidence that gives us!

Now move from imagining to believing. Believe that we can live our lives on purpose because we were made for a purpose.

We are God's masterpieces. He has created us anew in Christ Jesus so that we can do the good things He planned for us long ago. (Ephesians 2:10)

Making Time to Pray

With so many competing time demands, why should we pause to seek the Lord in prayer? Our lives have become overloaded with activities. Our children are highly programmed with school, sports, music, dance, and other activities. Of course, the parents are also impacted by their busy schedules. We are tethered in new ways with cell phones, and we now have the internet to compete with TV for our time. So, when is there time to pray?

Prayer honors God, builds our faith, and helps us see things from the Lord's perspective. Regular prayer time is essential to our spiritual growth. Unless we build it into our schedule, prayer can become an afterthought, something that is nice to have instead of a soul-feeding essential. We owe it to ourselves and God to make the time for prayer.

Prayer honors God and is one of the most important things a Christian can do. It is a time when we communicate with God and should be taken very seriously. Prayer is done by those who trust the power of God and use it to praise Him. Adoration for God can enable us to be continuously aware of His presence, creating a desire to punctuate our days, hours, and minutes with the communion and fellowship of prayer.

Prayer teaches us. While we may earnestly desire God's glory, and we may pour our lives into serving others for His sake, we still, at times, allow our own agendas to taint our prayers. So, we must pray with purpose. Allow God to search us, and ask that He cleanses us in the process. And when our sinful nature is revealed, repent. Confess mixed motives and invite God as we admit our shortcomings and missed opportunities. Once that's done, receive forgiveness and cleansing. Ask God to redirect our hearts and give thanks for all He has done.

Prayer changes things. Even when we think we're not getting through to God, know that He hears us. Stop looking around with human eyes, and observe things from God's perspective. Look at what He has done, is doing, and what He has promised to do in our lives and the world. Let God know that we agree with what He knows is best. Keep faith that our petitions align with His will.

The key to making time for prayer is to get up earlier than usual in the morning. Create quiet time early in the morning as this is when our mind is the quietest and the best suited for prayer. It is essential to begin the day with prayer to gain the strength to face all the temptations during the day. If we don't start the day with calmness, there is not much chance the rest of the day will be calm. Take time to give thanks for the blessings of the day ahead of us.

Once we have made the time, then make a commitment to keep a specific time for prayers. Think of prayer time as an appointment with God. Like any appointment, this includes having a specific time and place to meet Him. This is not easy, and the To-Do list will always be greater than the time we have to complete it. Let go of it as we enter into the time we've created for prayer. Protect His time as sacred space.

God is not sympathetic to those who do not choose to put Him first. It is true that He knows our struggles and has great compassion for our condition, and He is willing to help us deal with them. But we, first, must make an effort to be in a relationship with Him and with humility, seek His help. Be patient, and remain faithful.

Five Finger Prayer

1. Your thumb is nearest to you. So begin your prayers by praying for those closest to you. They are the easiest to remember. To pray for our loved ones is our sworn duty.

2. The next finger is the pointing finger. Pray for those who teach, instruct, and heal. This includes teachers, doctors, and ministers. They need support and wisdom in pointing others in the right direction. Keep them in your prayers.

3. The next finger is the tallest. It reminds us of our leaders. Pray for the president no matter how you voted, leaders in business and industry, and administrators. These people shape our nation and guide public opinion. They need God's guidance.

4. The fourth finger is our ring finger. Surprising to many is the fact that this is our weakest finger, as any piano teacher will testify. It should remind us to pray for those who are weak, in trouble, or in pain. They need our prayers day and night. We cannot pray too much for them.

5. And lastly, comes our little finger - the smallest finger of all, which is where we should place ourselves in relation to God and others. As the Bible says, "The least shall be the greatest among you." Your pinkie should remind you to pray for yourself. By the time you have prayed for the other four groups, your own needs will be put into proper perspective, and you will be able to pray for yourself more effectively.

Made on Purpose

Live life on purpose because it is defiantly not by accident. Knowing who we are and where we came from produces a momentous, dramatic difference in our lives.

We are not the result of some cosmic accident. Absolute and intelligent designs were involved in our uniqueness. The false account of life that things "just occurred," and we just happen to be here will lead us astray. When we believe we got here by chance, we will end up living our lives by chance and circumstances.

It may not seem like we think this way, especially when making life plans and setting our goals. But for what overall purpose?

When we know without a doubt that God made the universe and created us in His image (Genesis 1:27), we know we were made for a purpose. God is very purposeful in what He does, from every small thing to each major event in our life.

Imagine the confidence that gives us! Even without looking in a mirror, imagine we have all it takes to move out on the things ahead of us without a care of how to get it done or whether or not we'll be successful. God has purposed it so.

Now move from imagining to believing. Believe we can live our lives on purpose because we were made for a purpose.

"For we are God's handiwork, created in Christ Jesus to do good works, which God prepared in advance for us to do." (Ephesians 2:10). Each day is a blessing. We are called to love God and one another. That is our primary vocation. The reason we rise in the morning and the purpose of our life on earth is to learn how to receive God's love and then share it. God's gift of life to us each morning is a sign He has a mission for us that day.

A Little Inspirational Soup for the Soul

Inspiring Stories Retold

The Wise Woman

A wise woman traveling in the mountains found a precious stone in a stream. The next day, she met another hungry traveler, and the wise woman opened her bag to share her food. The hungry traveler saw the precious stone and asked the woman to give it to him. She did so without hesitation. The traveler left, rejoicing in his good fortune. He knew the stone was worth enough to give him security for a lifetime. But a few days later, he came back to return the stone to the wise woman.

"I've been thinking," he said, "I know how valuable the stone is, but I give it back in the hope that you can give me something even more precious. Give me what you have within you that enabled you to give me the stone."

Socks and Shoes

A little boy, about ten-years-old, was standing before a shoe store on the roadway, barefooted, peering through the window, and shivering with cold. A lady approached the boy and said, "My little fellow, why are you looking so earnestly in that window?" "I was asking God to give me a pair of shoes," was the boy's reply.

The lady took him by the hand and went into the store and asked the clerk to get half a dozen pairs of socks for the boy. She then asked if he could give her a basin of water and a towel. He quickly brought them to her. She took the little fellow to the back part of the store and, removing her gloves, knelt, washed his little feet, and dried them with a towel.

By this time, the clerk had returned with the socks. Placing a pair upon the boy's feet, she purchased him a pair of shoes. She tied up the remaining pairs of socks and gave them to him. She patted him on the head and said, "No doubt, my little fellow, you feel more comfortable now."

As she turned to go, the astonished lad caught her by the hand, looking up in her face, with tears his eyes answered the question with these words, "Are you God's wife?"

Prayer List

A very poorly dressed woman with a look of defeat on her face walked into a grocery store. She approached the owner of the store in the humblest manner and asked if he would let her charge a few groceries. She softly explained that her husband was very ill and unable to work, they had seven children, and they needed food. The grocer scoffed at her and requested that she leave his store.

Visualizing the family needs, she said: "Please, sir! I will bring you the money just as soon as I can."

He told her he could not give her credit because she did not have a charge account at his store.

A customer standing beside the counter overheard the conversation between the two, walked over, and told the grocer that he would stand good for whatever she needed for her family.

The grocer asked in a very reluctant voice, "Do you have a grocery list?"

"Yes, sir, I do. Here it is."

"Okay," he said, "put your grocery list on the scales and whatever your grocery list weighs, I will give you that amount in groceries."

The lady hesitated a moment with a bowed head, then she reached into her purse, took out a piece of paper, and scribbled something on it. She then laid the piece of paper on the scale carefully with her head still bowed.

The grocer and the customer's eyes popped in amazement when the scales went down and stayed down.

The grocer, staring at the scales, turned slowly to the customer and said begrudgingly, "I can't believe it."
The customer smiled as the grocer started putting the groceries on the other side of the scales. The scale did not balance. So, he continued to put more and more groceries on until the scales couldn't hold anymore. The grocer stood there in utter disgust.

Finally, he grabbed the piece of paper from the scales and looked at it with greater amazement. It was not a grocery list; it was a prayer which said:
Dear Lord, you know my needs, and I am leaving this in your hands.

The grocer gave her the groceries that he had gathered and stood in stunned silence. The woman thanked him and left the store. The customer handed a fifty-dollar bill to the grocer and said, "It was worth every penny of it."
It was some time later that the grocer discovered the scales were broken; therefore, only God knows how much a prayer weighs.

Given A Chance, What I Would Do

Differently

Talk less and listen more.

Invite friends over to dinner even though the carpet is stained, and the sofa is faded.

Eat the popcorn in the good living room and worry much less about the dirt when someone wanted to light a fire in the fireplace.

Listen to my father ramble about his youth.

Roll down the car windows on summer days after leaving the beauty salon.

Sit on the lawn with my children and not worry about grass stains.

Nuggets of Inspirations

Life is indeed situational. These nuggets are intended to

inspire during life's timely challenges.

Prayer is Universal

Prayer can be a way to determine who we are in understanding who created us, how we obtain our identity. May we find fulfillment in who we are by spending time in communion with Christ through prayer. Pray this prayer:

Dear heavenly Father, may my deliberate act of praying renew my relationship with You so that all will know and see You in me; and therefore, desire to seek You.

Cooperation with God

Faith, hope, and love are always somehow a gift-- cooperation with someone else, participation in something larger than ourselves. God invites us to continue to be good stewards.

We share our faith; we will find Him leading us more and more to people who are open to Him.

Understanding God's character and incredible love for us allows us to relax and trust Him in every area of our lives.

Finding Hope

Only God can turn a mess into a message, test into a testimony, a trial into a triumph, and a victim into a victory. This little saying offers a lot of hope during trying times for all of us.

Divine Love

I love myself solely for the sake of God. Now I just appreciate my origin and destiny in God. I am humbled by the incredible gift of divine love and feel my whole life has importance because of God.

Created for a Purpose

Heavenly Father, you created each of us for a purpose, to accomplish something special that will fit into Your plan. May we always be free to follow where You lead so that we can be guided and trained by You to fit in with the beautiful tapestry woven from the lives of all of us. Thank You, Father, for I am beautifully made. Amen.

Following His Lead

Whatever plans you have for me, Father, may I always be open to whatever Your will is for my life, and be able to accept the grace to follow wherever you lead me. I ask this in Jesus' name, amen.

The Skin You're In

Our relationship with Christ isn't just some set of spiritual clothes we put on to do spiritual work, to go to spiritual meetings, and then take them off. It's skin that we carry with us into every arena of our lives. Living for Christ is a style that we carry with us all day, everywhere, like skin.

Stretching

We are called to share in the infinite life and love of God. We are called by God to a relationship that is destined to transform us into His likeness. This is going to take some stretching.

To Dwell

The enemy loves it when we dwell on the past, simply because no matter what, it can't be changed. He loves it when we think about past failures, knowing full well you can't do anything about them. The enemy wants us to think about past damages to relationships, to ourselves, because we can't remove the hurt or shame they've caused. He wants us to dwell in that place instead of focusing on what we can affect, now and a future that has yet been written.

The most detrimental thing we can do to harm our spiritual relationship and walk with God is to dwell on the past. It is difficult to let go, but it is not impossible. The good news is that God forgives and forgets. He wants us to forgive ourselves and move on, to live life to the fullest in every way possible.

Keep our mind and heart steadfast on Him. Remain focused and deliberate in the Word and what He deems as truth. The past is there for a reason and has no place in our future. Trust Him to make it so.

Discipleship

The gift of our faith is not something we are to hoard for our own benefit; it is meant to be shared with the world. The beginning of the year is particularly a good time to begin to follow Christ's call to "Go out and make disciples of all nations." But if, by chance, we didn't start at the beginning of the year, now is the time to start. It's never too late or never too hard to share the living Word of God.

Real Praise

Real praise involves more than just lip service; it engages the mind and the heart. On the receiving end of praise are thoughtful, substantive declarations. By the way, praise will put a smile on the face of our spouse or friend, and especially God.

Routine Prayer Time

Regular prayer time is essential to our spiritual growth. Unless we build it into our schedule, prayer can become an afterthought, something that is nice to have instead of a soul-feeding essential. We owe it to ourselves and God to make the time for prayer.

Pathway to God

Almost anything we see or experience can be a prayer—a pathway or tool for turning into God. There is a whole spectrum of ways that can raise us to conscious union with God: passages of Scripture, repetition of words, silence, breathing, even suffering. Such experiences become springboards and passageways into God's presence. He's always there, willing and ready, no matter where we are.

His Answer

We often like to claim we don't know what God wants when, in reality, we do, and we just don't like His answer to our question. So, we pretend to be in wait.

Humbly Waiting

The essence of prayer consists in humbly waiting—in a childlike openness, expectation, and listening. To pray means we make ourselves present and available to God so that we are truly ready to open the door when Jesus comes and knocks.

Importance of Prayer

Prayer and ritual are kindling that sets our hearts burning. Whenever possible, (make the time) take time to sit in silence. Open your heart to the Holy Spirit, the gentle breath that ignites the kindling, and sets our hearts on fire.

Surrender is Difficult

Surrender equals defeat, failure, and unhappiness if we don't get our own way. We naturally feel we should have it all, should be on top, should do better. This struggle in our hearts between having our way and letting God have His way challenges us daily. Most often, we don't even realize there is a battle in our hearts to surrender our wills to Christ.

Silence is Good

Many of us feel uncomfortable with silence, but we need silence to hear the still, small voice of Christ calling us. Our minds and bodies need times of silence for self-reflection, prayer, and decision making.

Surrender to Faith

What faith gives us is the assurance that God is good, that God can be trusted, that God won't forget us, and that, despite any indication to the contrary, God is still solidly in charge of this universe.

Finding God

God doesn't abandon people just because an accident happened. He doesn't abandon people who are the victims of poor judgment or evildoers. He is always there. It's up to us to find Him.

Seeking God's Love

The darkness of our personal hells, perhaps more so than anything else, can help us understand the love that makes for heaven. It's this love that we seek in prayer. The love of God is not something to be admired; it is something to be seized and lived under.

Nothing about this journey is easy. The more seeking we do, the more we must remain diligent to the task, and the more paths of darkness we may have to endure. Yet, God's love always covers and is readily available, even when we don't think it is present.

Prayer is the place to seize God's love and is the place where His presence is what blankets us with love.

Life of Holiness

If we are faithful in little practices of love, in little sacrifices, in little interior mortifications, then we will become more Christ-like and build within ourselves the life of holiness. Holiness is only a very high degree of love. Let us all unite in helping each other to become holy.

A Battle of Wills

We sometimes fight God's plan when it challenges our own. Emotional attachment to our plans, or emotional resistance to God's, can obscure the wisdom of His ways.

Using Time Wisely

We fritter away time every day on silly Internet games, trashy novels, insipid television shows, and the like. And while we all need time to relax, we must be jealous of the hours we have been given here on earth to do God's work.

God's Word advises us to use our time wisely because He knows many things in life can distract us from what truly matters.

We must be wise stewards of our time, live with an eternal perspective that will lead us to do God's will. Remember that every minute counts.

We Have a Choice

It's hard when life kicks us in the pants. We always have a choice--give in to bitterness and anger, or pick ourselves up, dust ourselves off, and with God's help, start again.

Unexpected Answers

Isn't it amazing the way God answers our prayers, sometimes in the way we hope and anticipate, sometimes in other ways that serve us even better? Never be afraid to pray for something big or seemingly out of reach.

Good Relationships

Remember, evangelization is rooted in good relationships--with friends, coworkers, and people we meet every day. We are not in the numbers game. We want to help people discover the love and mercy of God right where they are.

Forgiveness

Forgiveness is a decision, not a feeling. We begin with God's command, we go through a grieving process if necessary, and when the time is right, we make an act of forgiveness. It is as simple as saying, "I forgive."

Growing in Love

God knows how hard it is to suffer. But He has created us to love. Our hearts are made for Him. We can only grow in this life by recognizing Him and loving Him more.

Letting God In

God is close, and his miracles are everywhere. He is with each of us on the road we must travel through life. He can work miracles for us every day if we merely recognize his presence and allow him to be part of our lives.

Knowing Who God Is

For those who believe in God and consider themselves converted Christians, thinking and acting more mature is a daily struggle. They want to act more like their elder brother Jesus Christ, yet have little, if any, idea on how to reach this lofty goal.

Bibliography

Zondervan, New International Version Bible, Copyright © 1973, 1978, 1984, 2011 by Biblica, Inc.™ Used by permission of Zondervan. All rights reserved worldwide. www.zondervan.com The "NIV" and "New International Version" are trademarks registered in the United States Patent and Trademark Office by Biblica, Inc.™

Inspire, Michael Bledsoe, 2001laugh@lists.crosswalk.com, 2001
Short stories shared with me by Joan Deneff, 2001

ABOUT THE AUTHOR

Ann Clay resides in Southern Illinois with her family. She enjoys reading, writing, crafts, traveling, and family time. She began writing in 1999 and is a member of New Life in Christ Church, O'Fallon, IL. Thanks to the support of family and friends, Ann shares her faith and heartwarming stories as a testament to her belief that Christ is the Living Savior.

Other Inspirational books by Ann Clay

Waving From the Heart, 2007, 2013

A Fresh Encounter, 2006, 2013

Faith in Ordinary Things, 2016

Tickle My Tummy, 2020